Vampyr

ISBN: 1981638806
ISBN-13: 978-1981638802

DEDICATED TO

My loving mother, Corina, for her continuous encouragement in everything I strive to accomplish. Thank you for always pestering me to write a book.

My father, Daniel, for taking care of me when I was not well and for his support in my many crazy antics.

My brother, Vlad, for being my best friend and for always making me laugh. I have never known anyone quite like you.

My life would not be the same without you three.

CONTENTS

Vampyr

ACKNOWLEDGMENTS

It's hard to believe that I've written my first book. This has been a dream of mine since I was a child living in Romania. I started writing short stories and poetry at the age of seven in my native language.

In 2001, my family won the VISA lottery and we moved to the United States. Within the year, I had an awkward grasp of the English language and began to switch my writing to English.

This book portrays many of the obstacles that I've overcome over the years. From immigration, alcohol addiction, depression, anxiety, and of course, love. However, the majority of this book is written with regard to my depression.

In 2011, I fell in love for the first time. I was young and life was beautiful, but I quickly fell into a dark depression paired with daily panic attacks. Still, I thought I had control over myself and so I tried my best to ignore it. I moved across the country from Florida to Ohio, enrolled in college, and tried to live my life to the best of my ability. But I wasn't okay.

During the winter of 2014, Ohio dealt with many blizzards and the infamous polar vortex. I too dealt with the blizzards inside my mind and succumbed to a darkness that I hope to never revisit. The depression that I thought I was handling, suddenly hit me like lightning and I became immobilized. I couldn't get out of bed most days, and if I did it was only to switch to the couch. I remember having to force myself to eat a banana every day. It would take me all morning to try to get it down and by then I was too tired to try to eat anything else for the rest of the day. My weight plummeted to the low 90s; I was skin and bones. My anxiety developed into nervous twitches that quickly became embarrassingly out of control, and constant shaking. My relationship suffered enormously and I had to move back home to have my parents take care of me.

My parents were wonderful, and I owe them my entire life for saving me during that time. They drove me to psychiatrists and therapists and talked me down whenever I had a panic attack. I was diagnosed with Clinical Depression and prescribed Prozac, which honestly changed my life. My dad would make me fresh smoothies every morning because I couldn't eat solid food. At night my mom, dad and brother Vlad, would all go on walks with me because they knew it was the only thing that made me feel better. Sometimes I would drag them out in hundred-degree weather in humid Florida, but they never complained or made me feel bad about it, and for that, I am so grateful.

After a few months, the Prozac kicked in and I felt so much better. I went back to Ohio, but that was the wrong choice. My relationship had suffered too much to be mended, yet we foolishly still tried. It ended so badly that I still cringe when I think about it.

I met someone else in the summer of 2015 and fell in a love that I can now only call obsession. He was terrible for me but I was reeling from the loss of my five-year relationship and still dealing with the depression that Prozac couldn't completely cure.

Once that ended, I moved back home to Florida and fell into a darkness unlike the first one. I started drinking every day and picked all the wrong people to surround myself with. I befriended the worst type of people who encouraged my toxic behavior. I fell in love with the wrong people and gave my heart to ungrateful men. I hope to never replicate the shame I felt then.

I somehow came to my senses and sobered up. I erased the people from my life who didn't bring any positivity. I finished school and graduated with my Bachelor's in Natural Resources. I found a good job in my field, spent more time with my family who I'd been neglecting after everything they did for me, and started writing more and more.

I started writing this book in January 2017 and quickly settled on the title 'Vampyr'. To me, depression has always felt like a vampire, which drains the very best parts of myself and leaves the worst. I've written several poems about it, some of which you will find in the pages of this book, so it only seemed fitting.

The words in this book are more than words. They are my entire soul and I gift them to you with hopes that they will help you through your own struggles. I am eternally grateful that you are holding this book in your hands.

The Beginning

One

Anxiety is
Floating on calm ocean water on a sunny day
Waking up to find yourself
In the middle of frigid roaring waves
Fighting off tentacles that drag you under
Into despicable depths
As you struggle to breathe
In a drowning universe
That stifles your dreams
And just like that
You wake up again
And everything seems fine
Until the next time
You drown again

Two

I would give up my sanity to have the happy ending
I know I'll never have.
But that's just it.
It will wake me in the middle of the night, make my heart ache, cloud
my eyes and scatter my thoughts into a universe of despair.
It will drag its knife through my chest, break open all the good parts of
me and leave only the worst.
It will make my days feel not my own,
make my mind foreign,
force me to lose my identity.
A metamorphosis.
I don't recognize myself.
I'll lose my sanity.
I'll lose it all.
And still never have my happiness.

Three

At the bottom of these muddled thoughts I have
there is something
I can't ever explain to any other soul
an idea that I can't pull out of my own brain
I fear that it will remain there until the day I die
It will forever be trapped inside my body
and nobody will ever know
what my soul so desperately wanted to say.

Four

Depression is what I imagine vampires
must feel like when they're thirsting for blood.
It's that disgusting miserable part of you
that you can't help or change.
You give in or you die of thirst.
And I can't figure out which is worse.

Five

I'm a madhouse on display for the world to see.

Vampyr

Six

I want to tell you that life is beautiful and sad.
It is angry, happy, and passionate.
It is all of our human emotions wrapped up into one beautiful universe
that we can hold in our fragile hands or keep in our weary hearts.
I want to tell you not to be afraid.
I know that you feel as if your world has been hit by hurricanes and
your heart by tornadoes, but you have so much living to do and it's
more beautiful than you can ever imagine.
Don't be afraid, because our fate can never be taken from us.
All that happens has already happened in the distant past, in that other
universe we lived before we came to this one.
The one where you found me, broken and alone, and made your home
into ours inside your heart.
I want to tell you to remember that fate is not fair.
It will break you, and mold your spirit into who you were
always meant to be.
The good and the bad, they both transform our lives.
Remember to feel the joy in pain, for it will force you down the road
you never thought you'd take, but the one you were destined for from
the moment of your lonely birth.
Remember, I will always be there, in the shape of who I've always been.
If you miss me, miss me with happiness in your heart,
not tears in your eyes.
One day you will recognize fate as the image staring back at you from
inside the mirror.

Seven

Is it possible that I died and I am now living through my hell?

Eight

"There is darkness in all of us." You always tell me not to worry so much about everything.

I always think, yes, but mine is more dangerous than most. But I can never bring myself to say it aloud. For fear that you would agree.

You know what the worst part of me is. You've always known and so have I. It's not the mistakes I made or the pain I inflicted upon our trembling hearts. It's not the screaming nor the selfish love we shared. It's this dark thing that lives inside me. It sleeps inside of me and it frightens me like nothing ever will. I know it will awake one day and wreak havoc on my life. If this isn't a nightmare, then what is? I know it could and will get worse one day. All the love I have will disappear and be swept away by the ocean waves that I always thought were cleansing me. I realize now that I am stuck. I am stuck here in the middle of the frigid ocean waters, where I swim but never make much progress. I'll reach the shore one day, I promise myself this every day. It makes me feel better but we both know it's not true. Maybe I'll be able to see the shore from a distance though, until this darkness that I both love and hate, will finally emerge and make me whole again. Just in a different way. I was meant to never feel, to never love, to never stay.

"Your darkness is a symphony."

Nine

Old photographs of my life make me feel like every part of me, every stage of my life, was played by some actor on a bright lit stage in a town I never knew. I smile so happily, so free in all the bent up photographs on the floor of my universe. I'm a swirling mess of memories, a tattered page from an old journal in his book, a frigid person now that I look back into the past. My eyes cloud over and I feel it all slipping away into the air. I reach and reach but the memories go off fluttering into the starry sky like butterflies. The wind blows them up, up, up and I remain here in the wilderness of earth. Among the concrete jungle of a corporate day dream as my dreams fade into reality. Out of the corner of my eyes I see the mountains looming in the darkest corner of my mind. They come closer every day and I can't seem to climb them when I approach. It's always avalanches of instability inside my own brain. It's the torture of my own words. It's my own thoughts that cripple my days. Simplicity would be so easy, to ignore all the open wounds that my soul patches up unwillingly. It's just my brain. It's always spinning, always reaching out for more, never satisfied. It is not a story that I know to write. It's a story that starts off in a language I once knew when I was young and finishes in a language I no longer understand.

Ten

The days haunt me with questions I can't answer.
I pull on the ones I love to make them stay with me
but I never understand why everyone is so
preoccupied in their closed off little cubicle lives.
It is a shame that life can't be lived the way we choose.
My art could mirror all of that but is there truly a point
in this creation if all roads will end at that same destination?
That same wooded forest in my mind where nobody ever visits.
It's all a mess, is it not?
Our lives are so much less than we think they are.
There is nothing serious about it,
just another day waking up on a spinning globe of madness.

Eleven

With the winter snow falling into blankets right beyond the window and the warm smell of home cooking drifting through the house. With my mother's kisses and my father's stories enveloping me into that beautiful memory. I wish I was there, stuck in time, in that very childhood moment. There was no past or future then. Today, there is and I don't want it. I want safety and happiness and nothing in between. The land of my doppelganger, for I do not live the same life as her. She is ever present and living in that room I loved, this I know. Oh, I just wish that we could trade places for one more day, like twins playing tricks on those we know. But every time I search for her, it is a game of hide and seek, which I always lose and she always wins.

Twelve

I was born in a small bright place in a land I can't forget but can't remember. I was born lost with my hands scrambling and my heart crying loudly. I will die lost in the place I can't forget but I will always remember. The time that the sunflowers were so high and I couldn't see or hear the world beyond them. That day that we took the trip to see the wild splayed out before us. The afternoon I heard the muffled sad voice on the phone telling me you'd died. All the moments when I swore I'd leave for the road beyond but never did. Every day I used to light a candle in your name as my father prayed for all of us as we stood there surrounded by the gold walls of the sun filled church.
It was too bright to comprehend.

You stood behind the white fluttering curtain and I remember how your feet peeked out and gave you away. You said "let's go to the woods" and I agreed that was where the fun would be. You chased me and I stole your white hat. You promised that I was important. Sometimes I think about the blood on your shirt. It makes me cry and I can't understand why I never understood before. Youth can be so ignorant and I wish that I'd known. I think about the loneliness you must have felt the night we said goodbye. Everyone had left you and it was now time to grow old. Alone.

It makes my heart scream inside of me when I can't remember your voice. All my memories are so fleeting and small. If I could make them grow perhaps I could understand it all some more. Maybe then I could see beyond the sunflowers.

Life is fleeting memories that haunt you while you sleep and while you wake. It's everything from birth that will haunt you to your death. I wonder if you ever felt that way.

Your ghost is my childhood.

Thirteen

I whisper miserable things in my sleep
and dream of the way the moon shines from inside my soul.
Unhappiness becomes a part of every smile, laugh and memory.
I try to push it away but sometimes I wish for it to stay.
I think I would be too lonely without it.
I want so badly to escape from inside my own skin
and to finally feel my soul free and floating through the world.
But I'm too drunk on the feeling of loneliness
to ever leave this place.

Fourteen

Everyone I know is either a fool or just another part of the charade.
I'd say "wake up" but sometimes I know that even I am half-asleep.
We will stay here.
All of us.
Trapped in this pretty little picture on the wall.
It's too much for most of us, to admit that we're unhappy, so we
pretend that we're okay with the game.
Not only are we okay but we are winning the game.
Most days I feel like the fly trapped in the spider's web.
I can see the world from in here, but I know I'll never be able to
escape.

Fifteen

The mundane moments of my days
pile up into the corners of my mind.
They become a clutter that I crave.
Sometimes I'm too depressed to be depressed.
I just want to be happy again but most days I succumb
to a numbness that I can't quite place.
I hate this feeling and the way I live but oddly enough
I think I'm finally starting to accept it.
Everyone tells me not to let it win.
But the thing is that it doesn't want to lose.
I wonder if we can coexist for the rest of my life?
Could everything I hate about myself
become something that I love?
Maybe all of our faults are just blessings in disguise.

Sixteen

The days pile up on top of one another in the dusty corner of our
room. I've never noticed them before but recently they seem to be all I
see. The tower of Babel of memories that never were.
I just wake up and wake up and wake up. I wake up never opening my
eyes to the days. I feel the shadows that await me in unknown times. I
feel the pull of my ancestors as they whisper unrecognizable words
between the realm of life and death. So I run for answers. I run to
psychics and to old friends to bare my soul.
I always come home emptier than when I left.
If only I asked myself.
I would answer with the truth.

The Journey

One

What if dying is just dreaming that you never wake up from?

Two

I am experimenting
on my own brain.
The pills that are supposed to save me
are the same ones killing me.

Three

I wish my brain was a puzzle
that I could put together with blurry pictures
and understand the entirety of it all
but it's really just lies in every way
no matter if I make sense of it or not
memories are not truth even when we believe them
we modify our dreams and the maps of our brains change so vividly
that we believe the lies we tell

Four

They look like people.
They wake up, drink their coffee, go to jobs they thought they'd like more than they do, come home, and do it all again and again and again.

They try to drain me, poison me with their false smiles, convince me that their lack of empathy is because the world is cold and so they must be hard to face it.

Allow yourself to become everything for someone even if they tear you down and rip out your heart with their own dirty hands. Even if they drown you in their tears and poison you with toxic love until your veins tangle and shrivel up into nothingness. Don't let the fucked up fuck you up. You are better than they are, I promise you.

They look like people but they aren't. They can't be human, these dirty fucked up beings that would rather see you die and smile when they see you struggle.

Don't let them snatch you up, these dark phantoms that kill love. They're shape shifters. Don't ever believe who they are because I promise you that they lie with every heartbeat, with every breath.

They look like people. They look like lovers. They look like friends. They look like saviors.

They are false ideals, dying memories, decaying loneliness.

Take another look.

They look like monsters, do they not?

Five

The summer usually greets me with depression.

Something about the longer days, the never ending sunshine, it gives me an anxiety that I can't comprehend. It traps me between the sun's rays and I can't move until the days are dark once more.

I can't stop the thoughts. The recurring loneliness, the existential fight my brain and my heart battle each day. It makes me dizzy and so I lay awake at night, thinking about all the other nights that were the same.

Sleeping on the couch rather than with you.
Sleeping on the beach rather than with you.
Except I was never sleeping at all.

Six

Sometimes I dream that I'm lost
inside of a vast building
with never ending doors
winding hallways
and stairs that I climb and climb
until I tire of exhaustion
and collapse into a heap of melancholy.

Seven

"Death is an old friend.
You couldn't die tonight even if you wanted to."
I gaze up at the stars while the ocean waves crash beneath our legs,
kissing our toes.
"Why do you say that?"
You always confuse me.
Your eyes stare off into a strange distance
that I don't believe exists in our reality.
"We aren't powerful enough to decide our deaths."

Eight

I shouldn't be alive
All those times I could have died
What kept me here?
Shackled into unstable ground
With my scrambled up mind

You tell me over and over
How I'm lucky to be alive
But my heartbeat sounds selfish
And I'm not feeling very lucky
With your hands around my throat

Not when vertigo daydreams turn into crippling nightmares
Not when I can't wake up without crying
Not when she watches my every move
from the corner of that dusty room

You tell me I'm crazy
But you fill my veins with blood each day
Just to drain me dry each night

You and I, we lost our chance to live
Lost our chance to die

So we are stuck in frigid limbo
Replaying memories that our brains have modified
so much that they're now fantasy

Vampyr

So yes, I shouldn't be alive
Not if all I dream of is you and the day I lost you
to the point of maddening addiction

Nine

There's always whiskey on my brain
on those frigid nights I spent alone
in that abandoned bedroom you forgot
where we'd smoke cigarettes
until our lungs burned from the inside out
and played broken records of songs that made me cry.
I wonder if I never met you,
how much happier would I be now?

Ten

At 9:00 am on Wednesday morning
You told me that you didn't love me
So at 7:32 pm on Friday night
I drowned myself in tears
Over an entire bottle of Jack
and too many Xanax
And met you in my dreams
where you loved me forever

Eleven

I should have died that night in the hospital
those vertigo dreams
they challenged existence
in the loveliest of ways
intoxicated my heart
in the faded sheets of a broken gurney

when heartbreak had fairytale endings
and my parents, the saviors, untarnished
with coloring pages surrounding my brain
and feelings of fire, of water, of air
on a fragile earth that held me in place
I should have died that night in the hospital

Twelve

I got lost in the fog on the way home
and part of me felt like I was
hallucinating on drugs that nobody
has ever possibly taken before.

Will my brain always feel like
a foreign book that I can't comprehend?

Thirteen

Do you remember those days
when you made me fresh carrot juice every morning?

The days I couldn't get out of bed
and if I did, I'd shake and wither into myself
or sink into a panicked frenzy of no escape.

I'd ask you
"Why is this so sweet?"
and you would reply
"I'm not sure, maybe you're just getting better."

But one morning
I saw you make it
I saw you add the honey with a smile.

And I knew that I had to get better
not for myself
but for you.

Fourteen

I left for a few months
while you stayed back and waited for me
to return to our home.

I was an anxious mess of self-hatred and fear
skin and bones
a hazy head full of clouded thoughts.

Sleepless nights on my parent's couch
doctors' appointments
and the hopeless drugs they prescribed.

I escaped through that awful yet beautiful book
that I picked up in a lonely bookstore
and read during sleepless vertigo nights.

It was about
an unhappy housewife
cheating on her loving husband.

I loved it up to the point where she killed herself
unable to find a way to live
within the reality she created.

My soul ached to be her.

That's why I got on a plane
went back to you

Vampyr

and broke your heart into innumerable jagged pieces
before departing once again
but this time
forever.

Fifteen

It's strange seeing a place you once loved
after so much time has passed.
It's often so different from the way you remember it to be
but yet there is still that sense of familiarity.
It's you.
Standing there in front of a place that is no more.
The memories are whispering in your ear,
telling you that this is real, yet you don't see it.
It's too sad to cry.
To heartbreaking to stay.
So you turn around and try to ignore the stories of your past
that call your name.

Sixteen

Depression is
driving to the market
to look at lemons
for 45 minutes
buying nothing
and walking out.

Depression is
forcing myself
to do strange chores
like putting that pen away
texting that person
I've been unwillingly ignoring
and washing the dirty spoons
in the kitchen sink.

Depression is
the little green pills
hiding in my cabinet
in my purse
in the car
I just can't forget
but sometimes I do.

Depression is
sleeping all day
dragging my body
to this faded couch
watching reruns of *Friends*

Vampyr

just to have some noise
in this too-quiet house.

Depression is
buying flowers for no reason
stocking the shelves with tea
borrowing too many library books
singing Bright Eyes in the shower.

Depression is
awkward,
terrible,
everything,
and nothing.

The Heart

One

"I miss you."
"You're always going to miss me."
I wish that wasn't true.

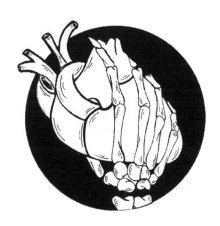

Two

"You'll get over it" everyone tells me. But we both know that's not
true. Every time I fall in love, I will think of you. Love is chaos. It grabs
you when you don't want it and just shakes you up
and stirs all your emotions.
Then, it falls apart and leaves you
to pick up the pieces of what once was.
The threat of loss seems implausible but love and loss are related and I
should know by now to not allow myself to fall in love.
I am too unstable to ever be loved the way I want.
It all ends in tears anyway.

Three

I woke up in the bedroom we used to live and I forgot who I was for a second. There is this distinct feeling that I remember, the strangest moment of my life, where I couldn't remember my name or how I got here. My entire life is a haunted life, the life of a ghost that will never be able to escape to the other side.

Four

Did you love me when my wrists bled red?
The night you found me crying on the floor
Whiskey on my dizzy brain
Whispering the name of a man who wasn't you
And pulling my own hair out
Dying over someone who wasn't worth a second glance
let alone my entire heart and soul
I'm sorry for ripping out your heart
with my greedy dirty hands
and letting it bleed on the floor
while you struggled to breathe
next to my weeping body

Five

When I drove away from you, I saw your image become a tiny speck and I kept looking even after you were long gone. It was goodbye, I knew it then but I know it even more so now. Every molecule of my being ached for you as I drove all night, but I somehow stopped myself from turning around and heading back to the lonely comfort of our home. Our love has become a phantom limb that attaches itself to my very heart. It will stay a part of me until the day that I die and even after. Until the universe swallows me up in its vastness and my body decays under the earth below. Until the God that might not exist beckons me to heaven. Until the rivers replace themselves with the tears of the raining skies. Until the sun burns out and kills us all. The only thought that keeps me from crying more than I already do is that I know we are both happy in a parallel universe, in an alternate timeline that we'll never have a chance to visit. This is our chaos, our hell, but don't let that define you. You are more than one person, more than one life, you are an infinite soul in a recurring universe and you will never be forgotten by the stars. No matter how much we hate ourselves or regret our choices, every moment of our life has had a purpose deeper than we could ever fathom.

Six

How could I let this happen?
I keep asking myself but my soul just stares back
from behind the mirror.

Seven

We didn't say hello with words.
I died a thousand times inside your eyes.
Our love imprinting on the celestial goddess that rules our lives.
The glimpse of memories I saw behind your smile eclipses on the
moon in such a lonely way that I swear we are both phantoms.
Our embrace composed music on that dizzy moon we pray to
every night.
The galaxies all hear it drifting through the cosmos.
They see our love as music that escaped this savage earth
we'll leave behind.
It paralyzes the oceans but still manages to sink the wandering ships in
unexpected storms.
Some days, when I hold you in the tightest of embraces, I can feel the
tentacles of your monsters dragging you down into the hellish depths of
"love" you crave yet you disown.
The darkest of nights with you are still the brightest of my life.
We are a never dying star, shooting across the sky but never ever
going out.
I feel the ghosts of our hidden truths follow us into our deaths.
You'll end it all with toxic candy for the sweet tooth you could
never satisfy.
The music of your life will play before your eyes and you'll smile
all the while.
Happiness is never found until the moment of our last breath where we
are reminded of all the love we knew but we let the day to day
steal the show.
You could and probably will escape to another wandering star inside
this dying universe.
I will too but first I must fall in love a couple hundred times.
I'll die in Paris on a rainy day with that fire in my veins and the glaze

over my eyes that you came to know so well.

But when our souls escape the vicious dullness of our dying star, will you turn to dust with me? Will you float within this ocean of emptiness with me? I'll carry you inside my heart until my very last breath when the God that I'm not sure exists reunites our energies once again. Until we become the dust that the universe uses to create the very life we lived and loved and hated under the brilliant sun we never really appreciated.

Eight

The stains of the moon hide the truth of your death.
All the loneliness I've ever felt won't create the beauty that I crave.
That's why I always dream of lovers who are ruined.
That idea of the star crossed lovers that are torn apart by death or life,
that's the only truth my heart will know.
Don't worry, you will learn.
The day will come when it won't hurt this bad.
The day will come when my soul remembers and forgets at the same
time that it loved you more than air itself.
Until then, let's pretend and watch the stained moon for signs.

Nine

Someone I once loved pulled me to the side, on that crowded New York street, right when the moon rose in the dirty winter sky and told me that true love was dead. I remember my chest tightening as your hands grabbed my face for the last time and your eyes stared into mine so deeply that my blood felt hypnotized inside my veins. The walk home through the park was a nightmare of my own muddled thoughts. Sometimes our love felt like Lazarus, always rising from the dead, always drowning in unexpected embraces. I always thought true love was dead until we met. Now I know it's real, it just doesn't last the way we hope it would. It doesn't make it false just because it fades away into the day rather than last forever and ever until decay.

Ten

Tortured souls recognize each other
and form into one in order to frighten the living
and allow their souls to breathe in the sadness of one another.

Eleven

You are the future nostalgia that will eat me alive.

Twelve

Pain is proof that love exists.
But what the hell am I supposed to do
with your ghost?

Thirteen

Love consists of mangled arteries
Twisted together into makeshift bodies
So you attach yourself to half a soul
Foolishly thinking they're whole

It's not until your veins both tangle together
And your dreams drown inside one brain
That you finally realize
Love was never meant to survive

Fourteen

There is hell inside of me
and heaven inside of you.

We are God
and Lucifer.

We love and love
until the chaos turns passion into despise.

Then I die alone
while you happily live forever.

Fifteen

I can't recall our love too well
but I do know that we were happy
for a few blissful moments in time.

I remember feeling
like the stars were holding me
among the sun and moon.

Waiting for
the comet
that was you.

Sixteen

It was weird when I had to learn to live without you.
So much of my soul was within you.
But there was none of you inside my soul.
You were always self-contained.

Seventeen

I collected souls with flaws
needles in their veins
voices in their heads
anger on their brain
men just like my father

Lies dripping from their honey coated words
distortions of human beings in love
but I'm no fool
I only loved you because nobody else would

I know that your tainted soul
was happy for a small moment in time
before your vices began to glow
brighter than love again

The Awakening

One

We are all victims of the fabricated realities we create.
You are conscious of my power.
I see it every time you look at me, even when you think I don't notice.
It fascinates you because it's so strong that you think you can touch it.
But I don't think you realize that my entire life
has been me flirting with disaster.
The idea of danger wakes me up in such a beautiful way
and I promise that all I want is to be the one who breaks your heart.
If you love me, you will suffer.
That I can promise you.

Two

True love is a facade but the unhappy pretend that they have found their soulmates just to keep the miserable searching until death do us all part. They are afraid of being alone, uncomfortable with the idea that life and death are meant to be experienced by our lonely soul and that no other person can ever make us whole or fill in those broken parts of ourselves.

Three

I finish that dizzy whiskey that's always changing the colors of the sky
making the moon swim, the stars drown
till it has me stretching out my arms to catch the wandering universe
above me

you bite my neck and I sense your hunger
craving my soul like a vampire does blood
wanting love but never giving in to the phantom
that follows you around

it's a carnal desire that only monsters are faced with
which is why it keeps leaving me wondering
if the monster is you or I?

probably both
let's be honest, look at the petty lies you tell yourself
look at the apathetic way I love
the haunted fires we hide

we sit in your car, motor running, your veins full of liquid love
your hands on my thighs
our lust in the air, drowning beneath a swimming universe
we decide that love doesn't exist
and then you drive me home

Four

Sometimes we don't have to be who we really are.
We are ourselves within ourselves.
We are we within our soul.
Hidden like phantoms.
It's difficult to tell if we are ghosts or liars.
We can pretend to others that we are genuine.
That we are true.
But we hallucinate happiness while we sleep.
And we lie while we speak.
Like the monsters that we are.

Five

All I have are hazy memories that feel made up.
Every day I ask myself what's wrong with me
and I know that only our dirty souls know the truth.
Liquid love, let it die I always plead, but it just takes over
and my brain forgets all the mistakes I make.
I always drown more the morning after, once the sadness kicks in
and I can't make myself forget. I can't feel anything, I can't cry or
laugh. I'm a ghost that you love but forgot even though my veins are
burned in your mind where you read them like a map. I always write
about you, me, or us but none of that exists, not today and not
tomorrow. And yesterday is a fucked up memory that flows through
brain waves of loneliness.

I just want to live until this kills me.
Something will, someone will, why not the toxic made up dreams
inside the books of my fucked up fragile mind?

Six

My entire life, happiness has been a ship that has constantly sailed away
from me in the opposite direction that I swam.
Today, I finally feel like I've caught up with it.
But it moves so fast and I know that I'll lose it soon and just fall back
into the miserable sadness that consumes my brain.
I'll once again become the vampire that I thought I cured myself from.
Happiness is pulling at me and I know that I want to follow it until this
ocean ends and the waves push me to shore.
Don't let me drown, again.

Seven

I am a wolf.
I am wild.
I howl at the moon every night when I can't sleep.
I stay awake and search the woods for the missing pieces
of my soul that I scattered long ago.

Eight

Do you know that when people like you are born, the rest of the world feels it in a very strange and slightly awkward way that we don't truly acknowledge? I bet that when you were born, the earth stopped spinning for the smallest fraction, in disbelief that someone like you could truly exist after billions of years and all these earthly changes we don't really know for certain. My energy, swirling out there somewhere in the dusty universe, became brighter just at the new feel that the world took on. The very essence of humanity, of our consciousness, or mine at the very least, changed as your soul breathed in life for the very first time.

But you don't exist. You are what I am waiting for. What I hope for. What I want and need and so desperately crave but will never encounter because the world is a chaos unlike what we think and our love only exists in hazy dreams and earthly feels.

Nine

Don't use love as bait
it will end up catching you too
and you'll tangle in the dirty net with me
unable to escape the grasp
of all you tried to get away from.

Ten

Once you've been awakened you can't go back to sleep
you will lay in cluttered beds of chaos
in the hazy illusion that you can go to sleep
you ask questions of the future and the past
but never of the present

asking what you cannot speak or think
you say "the past, it snatches at me with its withered hands.
and the future smirks, tells me I know what I don't know."
but when the moment comes
and you can no longer sleep
you will have to live

even when death sleeps in bed besides you
you will live without breath, without beats, without blood
if you've been awake, you're never leaving
if the earth pulls you back into its womb
and the sky, it looms on over you
you can know you have the future and the past
and the answers were always in your thoughts

because we always know what we don't know
once we've awakened from the slumber of our lives

Eleven

I'd give absolutely anything to be able to leave this town, this reality,
this restless body behind.
I would wake up tomorrow and head to the airport,
fly to a distant land that I never touched the soil of with my dirty feet,
and wait under that willow tree for my one true love.
The one who will see me and know my true worth, and kiss me until
the moon sets and the sun rises.
The saddest part of this is not that I will never go,
it's that you don't exist.
My one true love is the saddest lie I've ever known.

Twelve

"You were the sun, I was the moon, how can I go on without you?"
I cry into my hands, just like I have so many times already today.
Your ghost materializes in front of me and this time I know,
I've really lost it.

"Why do you cry?"

"Because the sun has abandoned me. My life has become the darkness
that I have always so desperately tried to get away from."

"If you cry because the sun has gone, the tears won't allow you to see
the stars above. Wipe your eyes and don't let this moment define you."

Thirteen

Love without obsession
to the point of maddening addiction
is not love at all.

Fourteen

"If you love me, don't let go".
But that's not the way this works.

Fifteen

You inject yourself with poison
just to calm the oceans in your brain
but don't you realize by now
that you're not swimming but drowning?

The Metamorphosis

One

I understand what it's like to have a heart made of charcoal.
We burn with desire for lovers that barely smolder.
I think the problem is that I love too much.
I love so much that I don't understand
that love itself is broken.

Two

The chaos in me is the chaos in you.
I feel your love through my own veins, like blood but more beautiful.
It flows through my veins in such a desolate way but it craves you even
when I wish it didn't.
I think I know how you feel.
I've lived and died within myself.
I've loved and lost within my soul.
I'm reading all the scars on my soul
and hallucinating happiness.

Three

Every time she smiles, it's a hypnotizing sadness that abducts the
thoughts from your brain. Like Medusa, she turns you to stone with
dead eyes and wraps your compliant body in her snakes, slowly twisting
your organs into a bloody pile, kissing away your soul into midnight
where it can fly but never escape.

You are but an ever-dying star in her universe.
The galaxy will continue to expand, the sun to burn, the planets to
align, even once your light burns out.

Maybe once you turn to stardust, you can whirl together through the
universe, your energies feeding off each other
as you float into that strange eternity.

But for now,
loneliness sounds happier than love.

Four

I dream of snakes.
They crawl through my brain.
Make their way out through my heart
as they eat away the rotting feelings I have left.
The decaying memories of you.

Five

The first spell
I ever performed
was making you fall in love
with the smile on my face
before you saw the sadness.

Six

These pills, they make me numb.
But without them, it feels like my brain
is dying inside my mind, my heart inside my chest,
my soul inside this makeshift body of memories and
crippling nostalgia of times that weren't good enough.

Times that I've built up inside my head.
With this realization, I can live.
At least for a little while.

Seven

The very idea of forgiveness
means that you've given someone
the power to hurt you.

I'd rather not hurt like this over
people who don't deserve even
the smallest pieces of my heart and soul.

I'd rather not forgive you
if it means I'm always hurting.
But I do forgive, me.

Eight

I know that even on the
midnight shores of some quiet beach
I'd still be lonely
still feel the pull of the waves
the depression strangling me
into an empty abyss
an oblivion of haunting anxiety
but at least I'd be away from you,
and these crippling memories of ruined obsession

Nine

I'm writing poetry in my dreams as I enter the home
where our love was born.
Today, I was in that blinding sunlight, looking up at the sky, and in an
instant, every molecule in my body knew that today is the day
the world ends.
But that moment never came.
I know that every second is my last, yet it never is.
Just like I knew you were the love of my life,
but you weren't.

Ten

"I feel as if I forgot who I was before all of this happened".
You thoughtfully tell me over the static phone.
"But now you can be anyone you want to be.
You can finally be you."

Eleven

I suppose that you and I, like others before us, have come through fire and ice, have had love erupt from the loneliest nights our hearts could take, have had life become the phantoms that our souls always knew we would be.

Love goes wrong, it crashes out at sea like a ship we chase but can't ever reach. We drowned each other in freezing waters, pulled each other down to the depths of the frigid waters where nothing but monsters can live. Most days I simply wish that I could drown but the ocean is unfair and the waves just push our bodies to shore every night.

I've had too many nights where I felt the whiskey in my veins more than the love I should have felt. I've realized that I don't love anyone quite as much as I love you but love isn't a reason to stay.
I'm happiest alone.

Happiest when it's just me and nobody else.
Nobody can save me.
Not even you.

Twelve

Some nights I thirst for real blood.
Those frigid ones where I dream of floods.
"You are a succubus, a deadly creature
that evaporates the very life from me."

I wanna know this time.
Are you still waiting for the climb?
I wanna know this time.
Do you still think of me in the summertime?

If monsters live and die within us all,
is the best part of us waiting in the waterfall?
You know the one, where we first kissed.

Where my very soul missed
the best part of us that ever was
back when you loved me just because.

Thirteen

Ohio is
a faded old love note
that I hide in my books.

Ohio is
an Amish picnic basket
you gifted me in July.

Ohio is
the therapist's office
where I fell out of love.

Fourteen

Depression always knocks
on my door
I don't let it in
yet, somehow, we always
end up here
on this faded couch
holding senseless conversations.

Fifteen

No, we can't stop
the celestial mistakes
that we were born to make.

But we can
pick up pens
and drip their ink
on paper, on skin.

Because nothing else
saves you
quite like poetry.

Sixteen

I want to write
something hopeful
so that you hold in your hands
words that make it easier to breathe.

But the best parts of me
are also the worst
and sometimes
no, most times
there's a war
happening inside of me
and even after all this time
I don't know which side
is winning.

So, if there's a war
inside of you, too
just let it happen
and realize
that even that
which you hate
about yourself
has some magic
that I hope you one day see.

The End

ABOUT THE AUTHOR

Natasa Ghica is a twenty-five year old Romanian writer who lives in Orlando, Florida. She works as an Environmental Scientist during the day and writes her heart out during the midnight hours. This is her first book, which she wrote about her struggles with depression, anxiety, and love. For more writing from her, you can visit her poetry page at www.instagram.com/ramblingsofamadromanian

ABOUT THE ARTIST

Malina Uami is a Mexican illustrator born in Puebla, Pue. With a strong reference from Tim Burton, she lives in love with dark and gloomy illustrations and stories. She tries to express her vision of the world with a balance between cute and dark. For more illustrations from her, you can visit her Instagram at www.instagram.com/malinauami

Vampyr

Made in the USA
Columbia, SC
17 August 2022

64855330R00057